KINGFISHER
READERS

Sharks

Anita Ganeri

KINGFISHER
NEW YORK

KINGFISHER
LONDON & NEW YORK

Copyright © Kingfisher 2012
Published in the United States by Kingfisher,
175 Fifth Ave., New York, NY 10010
Kingfisher is an imprint of Macmillan Children's Books, London.
All rights reserved.

Distributed in the U.S. and Canada by Macmillan,
175 Fifth Ave., New York, NY 10010

Library of Congress Cataloging-in-Publication data has been applied for.

Series editor: Thea Feldman
Literacy consultant: Ellie Costa, Bank St. College, New York
Text for U.S. edition written by Thea Feldman

ISBN: 978-0-7534-6905-7 (HB)
ISBN: 978-0-7534-6906-4 (PB)

Kingfisher books are available for special promotions
and premiums. For details contact: Special Markets
Department, Macmillan, 175 Fifth Ave., New York, NY 10010.

For more information, please visit
www.kingfisherbooks.com

Printed in China
9 8 7 6 5 4 3 2 1
1TR/0712/UG/WKT/105MA

Picture credits
The Publisher would like to thank the following for permission to reproduce their images. Every care has
been taken to trace copyright holders. However, if there have been unintentional omissions or failure to trace
copyright holders, we apologize and will, if informed, endeavor to make corrections in any future edition
(t = top, b = bottom, c = center, r = right, l = left):
Cover Alamy/Imagebroker; Frank Lane Picture Agency (FLPA)/R.Dirschler; Pages 4–5 Photolibrary;
5b Alamy/Stephen Frink Collection; 7 Photolibrary; 8b Photolibrary; 10–11 FLPA/Norbert Probst;
11t Nature Picture Library/Alex Hyde; 12 Alamy/Mark Conlin; 13t FLPA/R.Dischler; 13b FLPA/R.Dirschler;
14 Photoshot/NHPA; 16 Alamy/Imagebroker; 17 Alamy/ Jeff Rotman; 18 FLPA/Norbert Wu/Minden;
19 Photolibrary; 20 Nature/Doug Perrine; 21 FLPA/Flip Nicklin/Minden; 22 Alamy/Michael Patrick O'Neill;
23 Alamy/John Warburton-Lee; 24 FLPA/Stephen Belcher; 25 Photolibrary; 26 Alamy/Peter Alexander;
27l Alamy/Peter Arnold Inc.; 27r Shutterstock/Dennis Sabo; 28–29 Photolibrary; 28b FLPA/Pete
Oxford/Minden; 29b Alamy/Greg Vaughn.

Contents

Meet the shark

Sharks are fish that live in seas and oceans around the world. There are more than 450 different **species** of sharks. They come in many colors, shapes, and sizes. Some are sleek hunters that speed through the water in search of their prey. Others are giants that feed on tiny sea creatures.

Did you know?

The biggest shark is the whale shark. It can be up to 49 feet (15 meters) long. That is as long as eight adult humans. The smallest shark is the dwarf lantern shark. It is only half a foot (16 centimeters) long, about the size of a pencil.

In this book, you will find out all about sharks. You will see how they swim, what they eat, and how they are born. And you will find out about their super senses. Get ready to meet the shark!

The mako shark has a powerful, **streamlined** body. It is one of the fastest swimmers and hunts fish, squid, and other sharks.

The sawshark has a flattened body and spends most of its time on the sea bed. Its long snout has sharp teeth on the outside.

Megalodon

Sharks of the past

Sharks have been swimming in the seas for more than 400 million years. By the time the dinosaurs appeared, sharks had already been around for 200 million years!

Stethacanthus was an odd-looking shark that lived about 350 million years ago. It had a patch of small teeth on top of its head and on one of its fins. No one is sure what these teeth were for, but they may have been useful in **self defense**.

Stethacanthus

Megalodon was a meat-eating shark that probably died out about one and a half million years ago. It grew to be about 39 feet (12 meters) long—four times as long as a mako shark. Its jaws were lined with razor-sharp teeth. It probably hunted whales and dolphins.

Fossils

Our knowledge of **prehistoric**, or very old, sharks comes from fossils. People have found many fossils of sharks' teeth. This includes teeth from Megalodon that are as big as human hands.

Where do sharks live?

Sharks live in seas and oceans all over the world. Most are found in warm parts of the Atlantic, Pacific, and Indian Oceans, but a few live in the cold oceans near the North and South poles. Sharks live in every part of the sea, from shallow water to the deepest depths, and from rocky shores to coral reefs.

Did you know?

Most sharks live in salty seawater, but a few can also survive in the **fresh water** of rivers. Bull sharks swim hundreds of miles up rivers.

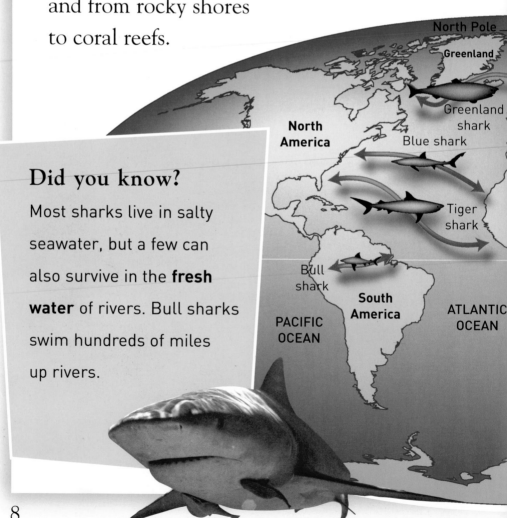

North Pole

Greenland

North America

Greenland shark

Blue shark

Tiger shark

Bull shark

South America

PACIFIC OCEAN

ATLANTIC OCEAN

The Greenland shark lives further north than any other type of shark. It is found in the cold, deep water of the Arctic Ocean around Iceland and Greenland. In the winter, the ocean freezes over and the shark survives underneath the ice.

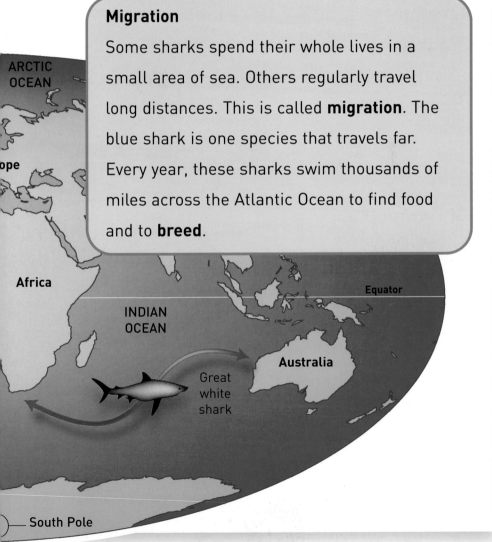

Migration

Some sharks spend their whole lives in a small area of sea. Others regularly travel long distances. This is called **migration**. The blue shark is one species that travels far. Every year, these sharks swim thousands of miles across the Atlantic Ocean to find food and to **breed**.

ARCTIC OCEAN

ope

Africa

Equator

INDIAN OCEAN

Australia

Great white shark

South Pole

Shark bodies

A shark's body is perfectly designed for living in the water. Many sharks have a streamlined shape for fast swimming. Their bodies are thicker in the middle, and **taper** (get more narrow) at the head and tail. Sharks have many other body features that help them survive in the sea.

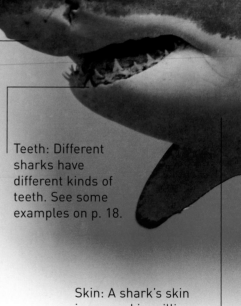

Jaws: A shark can move its upper and lower jaw. This helps it grab food.

Skeleton

Many fish have hard bones. But a shark does not. Its skeleton is made from rubbery **cartilage**. This makes the shark's body very **flexible** as it swims.

Teeth: Different sharks have different kinds of teeth. See some examples on p. 18.

Skin: A shark's skin is covered in millions of tiny, teethlike scales.

10

Did you know?

If you rub a shark's skin from back to front, it feels very rough. People once used sharkskin as sandpaper. This photo shows the scales on a shark's skin close up.

Dorsal fin: This helps the shark keep upright and balanced in the water.

Tail: The tail powers the shark through the water.

Gills: These allow the shark to breathe. As the shark swims, water flows over its gills. Oxygen from the water passes into the shark's blood and is carried around its body.

Pectoral fins: These help the shark to steer through the water.

Shark colors

Why are most sharks pale blue or light gray? These colors make them difficult to see in the water, so they help sharks to hide from their prey. Blue sharks, like this one, are dark blue on top and light blue underneath. If you look at a blue shark from above, it blends in with the dark sea bed. From below, it is hidden against the bright surface of the water.

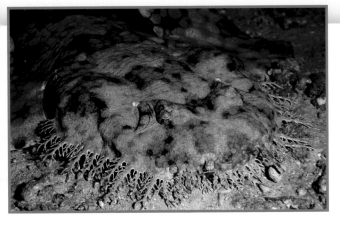

This wobbegong is perfectly hidden on the sea bed.

A wobbegong is an unusual-looking shark! It has a flat body and skin that has patches of color. The shark lies perfectly still on the sea bed, waiting for a tasty fish to swim by. Its shape and color blend in with the sand, rocks, and seaweed. By the time a fish notices the wobbegong, it is often too late because the shark has snapped it up.

Did you know?

Large, dark spots help keep a young leopard shark safe from larger predators. The spots help it blend in with the rocks and sea floor.

On the move

When a shark swims, it moves its body from side to side in large, S-shaped curves. This pushes the water back around the shark's body and forces the shark forward. The shark uses its strong tail for extra power. It uses its fins to help it steer and stay upright.

Did you know?

The fastest shark in the sea is the shortfin mako. It can swim at speeds of around 43 miles (70 kilometers) per hour, about as fast as a racehorse can run.

A shark tail

Shark tails come in different shapes. Many sharks, like the tiger shark, have a fork-shaped tail that is longer on the top. Every tail, though, helps a shark move forward in the water.

Tiger shark

Swell shark

Great white shark

Thresher shark

Most fish have pouches called **swim bladders** inside their bodies. These pouches are filled with gas and they help the fish float. A shark does not have a swim bladder. Instead, it has a large liver filled with oil. This helps keep the shark light enough to float in the water. Cartilage is lighter than bone and that helps too.

Shark senses

Sharks have very good eyesight. Their hearing and sense of smell are excellent. They use these senses to find food and mates. A shark's ears are behind its eyes and look like two tiny holes. A shark can hear sounds up to nearly one mile (1.5 kilometers) away.

A hammerhead shark

Sharks' eyes

All sharks have two eyelids, but some also have a third. They close this when they bite into their prey, to protect their eyes from harm. Sharks that don't have a third eyelid roll their eyes back under their top eyelids.

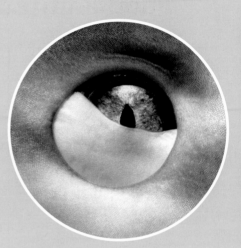

A shark's nose can smell blood from injured prey up to 1,312 feet (400 meters) away. A shark also has a special **organ** in its snout that picks up electrical signals from moving prey.

Did you know?

Sharks have such an amazing sense of smell that they can detect one drop of blood in a million drops of water. That's the same as being able to smell a drop of blood the size of a pinhead in a bathtub full of water.

Food and hunting

Some sharks are fierce predators that hunt fish, squid, seals, dolphins, and turtles. These sharks have large mouths lined with sharp, triangular

teeth. They swallow small animals whole, or take huge bites out of bigger prey.

This sand tiger shark's sharp teeth and powerful jaws are used for catching prey.

Sharks' teeth

The shape of a shark's teeth depends on what it eats.

Sharp, jagged teeth are good for biting and cutting prey.

Thick, flat teeth are good for crushing shellfish.

Long, smooth, pointed teeth are good for catching slippery fish and squid.

Not all sharks are deadly hunters. Some, such as basking sharks and megamouths, have huge mouths but tiny teeth. They are called **filter feeders**. They swim along with their mouths wide open, gulping in water and filtering out tiny fish and shrimp.

The basking shark swims with its huge jaws stretched wide.

Baby sharks

Some sharks, such as blue sharks and lemon sharks, give birth to live babies called pups. The pups grow and feed inside their mothers' bodies until they are ready to be born. They look like smaller copies of their parents.

Other sharks, such as Port Jackson sharks, lay eggs in the water. The eggs have tough cases to protect them. Inside, the **yolks** provide food for the growing pups.

This lemon shark pup has just been born.

Did you know?

Sometimes, empty egg cases wash up on the beach.
They are often called "mermaids' purses."

These egg cases have unborn swell sharks inside. The pups
will hatch in seven to ten months.

Port Jackson shark eggs have a **spiral** shape.
The mother wedges them into cracks in
rocks where they take between six and
nine months to hatch.

Some sharks, such as mako sharks, grow from
eggs that stay inside their mothers. The pups
grow inside the eggs, feeding on the yolks
until they are ready to hatch and be born.

Whale sharks

Everything about the whale shark is ENORMOUS! It is not only the biggest shark, it is also the biggest fish in the sea. This giant can grow up to 59 feet (18 meters) long and weigh about 45,000 pounds (20 metric tonnes)—as much as three African elephants. It also has the thickest skin of any animal. The skin is like tough rubber and can be up to 4 inches (10 centimeters) thick.

This human diver is tiny beside the whale shark.

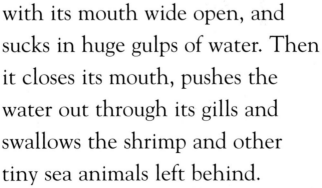

Whale shark facts

Habitat: mainly open ocean

Color: gray-blue with white spots and stripes on top, pale underneath

Diet: shrimp and tiny sea animals

The whale shark swims in warm oceans, just below the surface of the water. Despite its huge size, the whale shark is not a fierce hunter. It swims along slowly, with its mouth wide open, and sucks in huge gulps of water. Then it closes its mouth, pushes the water out through its gills and swallows the shrimp and other tiny sea animals left behind.

Great white sharks

The great white shark is probably the most famous shark of all. It is also the largest meat-eating shark in the sea. The great white shark has a powerful, streamlined body, a pointed snout, black eyes, and a tall, pointed fin in the middle of its back.

Did you know?

The great white shark sometimes lifts its head out of the water to see what is around it. This is called "spy hopping."

A great white shark can leap out of the water.

Each of the great white shark's teeth is longer than your middle finger.

Great white shark facts

Length: up to 19.5 feet (6 meters)

Weight: up to 4,480 pounds (2 metric tonnes)

Habitat: mainly near the shore

Color: dark gray, with a pale gray underside

Diet: fish, seals, sea lions, dolphins

The great white is a fierce and dangerous hunter. It feeds on a wide range of sea animals, which it catches with its jagged, razor-sharp teeth. The shark shakes its head from side to side to bite off chunks to swallow.

25

Shark attacks

Some people think that all sharks are dangerous creatures that eat people. In fact, the chances of being attacked by a shark are very small. There are only about 80 shark attacks in the whole world each year and fewer than 10 people are killed.

Did you know?

Dead sharks can still bite! A man in Australia was driving home with a dead shark in his car when he had a crash. He was thrown on to the shark's jaws and was badly injured.

Shark safety

If you want to go for a swim where sharks live, don't swim in the evening. This is when sharks are more likely to be hunting for food. Make sure you choose a beach that has a lifeguard. Some beaches even have shark-spotting helicopters and planes.

A surfer seen from below can look like a sea turtle to a hungry shark.

A sea turtle seen from below.

Sharks can see better from a distance. Sometimes, a shark bumps an object with its nose to find out what it is. Then, the shark swims away. But, up close, a person may look like a seal or a turtle. So the shark attacks, thinking it has found a tasty meal. The sharks that are most likely to attack people are the great white, bull, and tiger sharks.

Sharks in danger

Every year, people kill millions of sharks. Some people kill sharks for their meat. Others chase and hunt them for sport. Fishing boats often catch sharks in their nets accidentally. Chemicals from farms and homes **pollute** shark habitats. All of these things are putting sharks in danger of extinction.

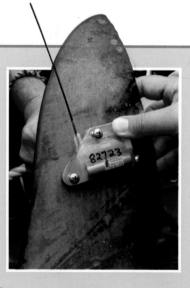

Tagging

Scientists put **tags** on sharks to follow their movements and study how they behave. Some tags are simple pieces of plastic, fixed to a fin. Others are like mini radios.

Scientists and **conservation** groups are helping to save sharks and their habitats. They help people

learn that sharks are amazing animals. In some places, visitors can go on boat trips to watch sharks. You can also see sharks up close in some aquariums.

Did you know?

Some sharks are killed just for their fins, which are made into soup.

Glossary

breed to have babies

cartilage a tough, rubbery material that makes up a shark's skeleton and is lighter than bone

conservation the act of saving the natural world and the animals and plants that live in it

filter feeders sharks that swallow water and filter the food out of it

flexible able to bend easily without breaking

fresh water water in lakes, rivers, and in ice that is not salty like seawater

migration a long journey made by many animals every year at the same time to find places to feed and breed

organ a part inside an animal's body such as the heart or lungs

pollute to make a place unclean and unhealthy

prehistoric a long time ago, before history was written down

self defense when an animal protects itself from being attacked

species a group of plants or animals that all share similar features

spiral a long, twisting shape

streamlined having a shape that can move easily through water or the air

swim bladders pouches filled with air, found inside many fish, which help the fish float. Sharks do not have swim bladders.

tags things scientists put on sharks and other animals to track where they go and what they do

taper to get narrower in shape toward the end

yolks the parts of eggs that provide food for the growing baby inside

Index